TO PARIS

Other books by Samuel Hazo

Poetry
Discovery
The Quiet Wars
Listen with the Eye (with photographs by James P. Blair)
My Sons in God
Blood Rights
Twelve Poems (with intaglios by George Nama)
Once for the Last Bandit
Quartered

Translations
The Blood of Adonis (poems of Ali Ahmed Said)
The Growl of Deeper Waters (essays by Denis de Rougemont)

Criticism
Hart Crane: An Introduction and Interpretation
(Reprinted and enlarged as *Smithereened Apart:*
A Critique of Hart Crane)

Fiction
Inscripts
The Very Fall of the Sun

Chapbooks
Entries from the Interiors
Shuffle, Cut and Look

TO PARIS

Poems by Samuel Hazo

A NEW DIRECTIONS BOOK

ACKNOWLEDGMENTS
Grateful acknowledgment is made to the editors and publishers of magazines and
books in which some of the material in this volume previously appeared: *The
American Scholar, John Berryman Studies, Contemporary Quarterly, Counter/
Measures, For the Time Being, The Hudson Review, The Nation, New Directions in
Prose & Poetry 41, New Letters, The Ontario Review, The Poetry Miscellany, Poetry
Northwest, Slow Loris Reader,* and *Tar River Poetry.*

Portions of this book appeared as separate publications and are reprinted by per-
mission of the publishers: "Radius" in *Symbolism and Modern Literature: Studies in
Honor of Wallace Fowlie* (Copyright © 1978 by Duke University Press, reprinted by
permission of Duke University Press); "Regardless" and "Saltpulse" in *Three Rivers
Poetry Journal* (Copyright © 1977 by Three Rivers Press, reprinted by permission of
Three Rivers Press.)

Library of Congress Cataloging in Publication Data
Hazo, Samuel John.
   To Paris.
   (A New Directions Book)
   Poems.
   I. Title.
PS3515.A9877T6 1981   811'.54   80-22685
ISBN 0-8112-0787-0
ISBN 0-8112-0788-9 (pbk.)

New Directions Books are published for James Laughlin
by New Directions Publishing Corporation
80 Eighth Avenue, New York 10011

Contents

Foreword

With a writer as well known as Sam Hazo there is only one reason for a Foreword—to say thanks.

As director of the International Poetry Forum in Pittsburgh, he has created an audience for poetry which can be seriously compared with the thronging, intent listeners who made the Ninety-Second Street YM-YWHA in New York famous a generation ago.

As critic and man of letters he has kept his head in a time when it was widely fashionable to have no head—no values and no standards.

And as poet himself he has faced the contemporary problems of poetry with intelligence and sense.

These last two achievements are evident in this book—in his understanding of the experience of Paris in the years after the First World War and in his handling of the problem of the speaker in modern verse.

For years now "Paris in the Twenties" has been a fashion-magazine, best-seller, travesty of the truth. Paris of those years has been famous because of the night life on the Butte, not because of the master work of Picasso and Stravinsky and Joyce and Rilke and *In Our Time*—a great decade of almost unexampled creativity. Hazo knows better because he has read the books and listened to the music and seen Bill Rubin's exhibit of Picasso in the Museum of Modern Art. The proof is in these pages.

And so is his professional perception that one of the problems of the art of poetry at this turn of time is the problem of the speaker. Dante's "I" needs a Dante to manage it. Homer's "He" needs not only Homer but Troy and those dissolving figures among the god-delighting clouds. Hazo, like others, has found ease to speak in the "You" who is both "He" and "I"—Rimbaud's "You".

Ce soir-lá, vous rentrez aux cafés éclatant,
Vous demandez des bocks ou de la limonade . . .
On n'est pas sérieux quond on a dix-sept ans. . . .

Archibald MacLeish

Anne's

Radius

Salted by rain, the ocean
  roughens into clashing circles.
They widen, arc by arc,
  toward predictable collisions
  with the shores.
              After they shatter,
  you remember you're the core of every
  circle that begins with you.
Like any hub, you center
  six-times-sixty spokes
  that finger outward for the poles,
  the centuries, the stars.
                 You intersect
  a candled dinner at the Ritz,
  the oiled sculpture of a riflestock
  against a hunter's shoulder,
  hummingbirds blown wild as ashes
  in a hurricane.
             If poetry is traveling
  without a ticket, you're a poet.
You follow every radius
  as far as you can dream.
             No
  matter where your body's been
  or where it goes or what
  it leaves you to remember, all
  your dreams precede you . . .
Before the astronauts, you left
  your bootprints on the moon.
Predating all the conquerors, you saw
  the cedars of the Lord.

The way
you danced through Paris in your sleep
makes Paris dance that dream
awake each time you summer there.
Fulfilling all your prophecies
by running into them, you're like
the bull's-eye of a world within
a world around a core that opens
in the always present to the never
very far.
When you stand still,
you're one of many radiating suns
until the air becomes the sum
of circles interlocked like zeros
on the sea.
Each circle's center
never moves.
Each center's circles
never stop.
To be both one
and all is what they teach you.
Wait, and the rings will reach you.

I

An America Made in Paris

Signing the Air

You dream you've used this tool
    for sixty years.
                Even Pablo
    liked the way it left your signature
    in fissures that denied your fingers.
All your bronze or marble sculptures
    grew from clay.
                You told Picasso,
    "Ruiz, if slime was adequate
    for God, then clay is adequate
    for me."
                Paint was his clay.
Blue paint was all he could
    afford in that cold "period"
    near Sacre-Coeur.
                Instead
    of models, Pablo posed some
    Montmartre whores to be
    Les Demoiselles d'Avignon.
Whores were cheap for men who pooled
    their francs and lived for months
    on sweet potatoes, leeks
    and long, stale loaves.
You called yourselves the wards
    of Paris.
                But so did everyone:
    Armenians, monarchists, expatriates
    like Joyce, Americans who came
    to find America in France
    and did and wrote it down
    in books and took it home
    with them.

No matter where
you went from Montparnasse to Rue
Lepic, something was happening.
Each Sunday, Hemingway would stop
or Nadia Boulanger with Archie
and Ada MacLeish or Ezra Pound
with his cane.
Rodin patrolled
the Tuileries beside his aide—
a German-Czech named Rilke.
Modigliani painted and repainted
the same unsmiling ikon
with the breasts of Venus.
For you,
each model was a midnight bride.
Her name was Fun-without-a-face
or Headache-in-the-morning.
After
you found the one whose life meant
more to you than yours, the slightest
infidelity was like the mating
of hyena with hyena.
All
you remembered was the smell.
Married or unmarried, Pablo
never understood.
A Mediterranean
of the Spanish earth, he kept
his minotaur erect until the end . . .
Then, *fini!*
Your final day
in Paris dawned no different
than your first.
Croissants
and cheeses from Gruyere . . .

The sun's

a coppery shower.
You sip

black coffee.
You trace meandering

rivers of grain around
two knotholes in the tabletop.
Across the Seine, the Eiffel
Tower interrupts the sky.
The blue

south steadies the gray
north over Notre Dame.
You

swallow coffee like the sacrament.
The panorama's like a canvas
with the paints still moist.
You squint it into focus, smile
and sip as if the only thing
still left to do is fit
that sacred city in a frame,
then pencil in the lower right-
hand corner—very small—your name.

The Vigil

See?
      Of course, you see, see well,
see better than most.
                  But seeing's
not enough.
                  You're like the boy
who had no courage but the courage
of his eyes to say the naked
emperor was naked after all.
You paint what you see until
   you see what the paint sees.
Some painters build their paintings.
You discover yours when they
   discover you.
                  Most nights
you sit before an empty
canvas like a guard on post,
deciding what you just won't
do.
         That's all that painting
means to you: deciding what
is worth the paint or not.
Perusing Schiele's sketches or Picasso's,
   you learn their art from what
   they both left out.
                  Cézanne?
No different.
                  Hemingway learned
leanness from Cézanne, and Hemingway
stayed lean as veal.
                  You nix
experience.

          Experience deceived
Renoir.
        The two-sweet pink of all
those tubbed and tubby bottoms
sweetened with the years . . .
               Gauguin
drew better as he aged.
           You taste
his greens and browns.
        Dali?
An average draftsman but a clown
at heart.
        Compared with Goya,
he's a speck.
        Utrillo drafted,
but he drafted with God's eye.
And Schiele?
        His crazyquilts of hell
and all those models—drawn
as if their pubises were mouths—
were masterpieces from the start.

Some Words for President Wilson

Declaring war on Germany but not
   its citizens, he took no enemy
   for granted but Americans.
                             They
   crippled him.
                    After his stroke,
   he somehow kept his grin.
                          That,
   his pince-nez and his Presbyterian
   chin survived the lost
   election and the sag of normalcy.
Blanketed and read to by a wife
   rare men deserve, he thought
   of Princeton, Trenton and the years
   before Versailles . . .
                       He never guessed
   that he would be the final
   president to write his speeches
   out by hand.
                Or that
   the future he foresaw but never
   saw would happen differently
   the same and change its wars
   by number, not by name.

Napoleon's

Appropriate that near the tomb
   of Bonaparte, upended cannon
   barrels should defend the corridors.
This Corsican who loved artillery
   would surely have condoned such vigilance.
"Give them a whiff of grape,"
   he muttered once before he fired
   at a mob with scattershot.
                              To crack
   an enemy's defense he nixed
   direct assaults as rapes.
                              Instead,
   he concentrated all his cannonpower
   on the weakest of the weakest flanks
   of that defense until it cracked.
Accepting losses with a lover's
   shrug, he claimed that Paris
   could replace them in a single night.
At Waterloo, the rain, not Wellington,
   defeated him.
                              Unable to maneuver
   caissons in the mud, he damned
   the French, the English and himself
   to history.
                              That history engraves
   the upright cannonshaft that he
   erected in the Place Vendôme
   from all the melted guns of Austerlitz.
Centering the square, it scrolls
   in corkscrew chapters to its tip
   a bronze procession of the passionate
   in arms . . .

Outside the Ritz,
a newsgirl pedals by, her nipples
tenting a *Herald-Tribune*
T-shirt sweated to her breasts.
Tour guides and all the guided near
the pillar glance away from France
to study what is after all
quite clearly in a manner of speaking
also a piece of the tale of France.
Aroused and rising to a war
they think they'll win, a few
stragglers, squinting at their target's
front and flanks, change
suddenly to cannoneers and zero in.

White Silence

You work more slowly now.
It's not the years.
              It's
   how the years insist on being
   kept in mind that tires you.
You sit in death's lap and know it.
Years back, you imitated Georges
   Rouault, painting sundowns
   in the morning.
                    Now you reach
   for noons at midnight, and they're gone.
But still you reach . . .
                      Beyond
   your window you can see a pair
   of helicopters snoop like dragonflies
   for traffic clots.
                    A bird-chalked
   general goes on commanding
   from his rusting saddle.
                         Vapor shimmies
   from the manhole lids like steam
   from old volcanoes.
                     You'd love
   to paint the silence there.
                            Impossible?
No more impossible than making maps
   or sketching nudes.
                     What else
   are maps but studies in abstraction?
Whoever saw the earth from those
   perspectives?

Who christened Europe
green and Asia blue?
                          And as
for nudes, what are they but
complexities of light and lines?
You catch the light by painting in
    the lines.
                  Later, you erase the lines.
You feel the silence of the street
    that way.
                  You've walked those stones
so many times they talk to you.
You listen with your heels.
                              If you
could solve—if you could only
solve that silence with a brush . . .
To see is not enough.
                      You've seen
too much already, and you don't
forget.
            You even notice how
the recto-verso greens of dollars
reproduce the tails and heads
of maple leaves.
                    Half your
life is learning to express
that kind of trivial amazement.

Elegy for the First Life

Without your mate, you learned
  that love's the only cancer.
It kills by not killing.
You kept your attic stocked
  with what you chose together:
  pewter salad spoons, pepper
  grinders carved from sandalwood,
  suede scraps and railroad calendars.
Her favorite was a bathtub squared
  on four bronze claws.
You trucked it from Versailles
  for her.
                    Its porcelain peeled
  and cracked as small as puzzle
  pieces or large as separate states.
For years you mopped and swept
  and locked the attic like a shrine.
Your mopcords tufted down
  into a spinster's knot.
                    The broomstraw
  slanted from a thousand sweeps
  until you swung the handle
  like a hockey stick . . .
                    Once,
  even the dust was important.

Waiting for Zero

Confirming that the avant-garde
  can't wait for history, gray Hemingway
  reached Paris seven days before
the liberation.
        With Nazis near
the Place Vendôme, he freed
his moveable feast and waited
for the troops . . .
             Like Hemingway you wait
for snow before a January second
masquerading as the first of May.
The maple buds almost believe it.
Stallion dung around a pear tree
  thaws into its pasture smell
  again.
        Even a buried crocus
lets its periscope break ground.
So far, no snow.
          Whether
it will come or go is in
the winds of Canada.
            But you . . .
You act as if it's here.
          Your blood's
already down to three below.
Your shoulders chill and heighten
  in the winds to come.
         Remembering
the future as a fact, you turtle up
like any seed beneath the snow
or like a snoozing black bear

in the hills and wait for Easter,
wait for history . . .
                         But just suppose
the wait's too long and troublesome.
Or else suppose that Easter's
not enough—or not at all.
Which brings you back to Hemingway
in Idaho in 1961.
                         His feast
no longer moveable, his hunter's
eyes too sick to see, his future
certain to grow worse, he faced
the choice of waiting for the end
or not.
                         At last he thought
ahead of how it felt to be
the first to Paris.
                         Then,
he held the muzzle cold
between his teeth and bit and shot.

The Long Passion

Your paintings show us all
  born crucified.
                    Christian
or Jew, there's no denying that.
Accepting it is something else.
Accepting it and going on
  is something more.
                    You can't
  call any man a man
  who hasn't seen the nailmarks
  in his palms.
                Religious?
                     No.
You quit on planned religions
  when you learned to doubt.
                      If
  praying in a pew meant asking
  God to guarantee salvation
  in advance, you saw all praying
  as a bet, with God the pot . . .
For you a life to come must equal
  living at the peak and then
  exceed it.
               If not, why live
  to die?
                When you were young,
  you prayed and fasted for the truth
  until you understood why Protestants
  go mad, and Catholics sin,
  and Jews seem destined to lament.
At last you realized that you
  knew nothing more than anybody

knew since there was nothing more
to know.
                    Today you settle
for the nails.
                         Meanwhile, the nude
world waits for you to make
a bride of it.
                    Your paintings
prove that nothing's right beyond
perfecting what began with God.
And nothing's left but dancing
   on the deathbed of the world
   that's always yours for the discovering.
Surviving like the pawn that saved
   his queen, you tell the final
   bollixer to keep his question marks.
What says you're mortal?
                              Death.
What lets you be immortal?
                              Death.

All Colors End in Black

Once you were an actor.
Under the fake whiskers
  and the powdered hair, the man
  inside of you resented being lost
  in character.
          You faced new roles
  the way a man confronts
  the books he owns but hasn't
  read.
       Finally, you quit.
The audience was always *they*
  and never *you*, the roles
  demanded too much dying
  to yourself, and everything depended
  on applause.
          You saw your fate
  determined by a boo.
            Still,
performing schooled you to the value
of the hint.
       The unsaid word
was louder than a scream, the unmade
gesture could suggest an avalanche,
and tears held back were tears
that no one could ignore.
             That taught
you to avoid primary colors
on your canvases.
         After the first
dazzle, what's redder than red?

Even today you let your paler
   colors brighten as the watcher
watches.
            Pistachio intensifies
to peppergreen, apple to blood,
lemon to butter etc.
            Instead
of vomiting a rainbow, you underpaint
the necessary accident.
            Your *Horse*
in a Billiard Parlor shows
the horse more *horse*, the billiards
more intensely *billiards*.
            Your oil
of Tipasa makes the sky burst
white above an inch of desert.
One tree is all that punctuates
   the sand the way a navel tightens
   in and down the nakedness around it.
Somehow the whole savannah
   pivots on the peak of one small
   tree that has no reason to be there.
Or once you sketched a nude
   dressed only in a cap until
   the cap was all that anybody saw.
That kind of miracle is all
   you keep between yourself and history.
History says a painter's how
   he lived.
            And history is right.
Art says a painter's what
   he leaves.
            And art is right.
The miracle becomes a curse.
As long as all you yield
   to midnight is your shadow, you

21

defy the curse by seeing
what is always there and saying
so in colors.

          Only the dark
can stop you.

          Or yourself . . .

                    If you
give up, the dark's
already come.

          Lately, when you
sleep, you let the lights
stay bright.

          That way
the scale of colors hums alive
for you all day all night.

Understand the Highway,
Understand the Country

Driving relaxes you.
                    You like
    the solitude of long trips
    to nowhere in particular.
                    Next
    year you plan to drive due
    north until the last road
    stops in tundra—or south
    as far as Tierra del Fuego.
Why?
            So you can meditate in motion.
Steering down a road, you
    study how the windshield
    frames what's coming
    while the rearview mirror
    telescopes what's gone.
                    The side
    windows smear with presences
    you can't make out until
    they're past.
                    You move against
    the earth's swivel.
                    Later, you
    sweat to put that feeling into paints
    so that your pictures move—
    move while you look at them.
No wonder you're at odds with poets.
In your beginning was the picture,
    not the word.
                    Cave paintings,
    hieroglyphics—you see them all
    as stories for the eye.
                    Television,
    film, cartoons?

          Updated
     hieroglyphics, nothing more . . .
For you, the caravan of mile
     after mile never lies
     and never stays the same.
Driving anywhere, you're just
     a speeding witness to God's
     fresco, frame by frame: a boy
     walking a wall as if it were
     a tightrope over hell; two roofers
     shouldering a beam; an overturned
     Buick, its tires spinning
     to a dead roulette.
                    You let them
     memorize themselves like postcards
     as you go.
                    Maybe you will
     read them, maybe not . . .
                              Highwaying,
     you can look ahead, abreast,
     behind like some twinfaced
     divinity who sees in retrospect
     what's coming while the past
     just happens.
                    Or are you King
     Ulysses resurrected to repeat
     a trek between the world's
     absurdities and one man's
     luck?
                As long as driving makes
     you finally a maker of horizons,
     you survive like Cain in Babylon.
The heatwave in the distance
     bends and dances in the wind
     while you roll down the windows,
     slug your will and skill behind
     the wheel and steer into the chances.

The Next Time You Were There

After Paris, every city's just
  another town.
                    Elephants could roam
  the Metro, Marly's horses
  could invade the Tuileries, wishbone
  arches on the Seine could shatter
  under traffic, and Parisians could
  refuse to estivate in August . . .
Appearing every day in Paris
  would be Haussmann's Paris, still.
Abroad, you'd like to die the way
  you live in Paris, telescoping four
  days into three, feeling that your best
  is just ahead, protesting
  that you need more time, more time,
  protesting to the end.
                    And past
  the end . . .
                  But you exaggerate.
This capital you share with France
  is just another web—somewhere
  to breathe and board and be.
You bring there what you are,
  and what you are is nowhere
  any different.
                This makes
  the Trocadero just a penny's patch
  of grass, the Place de la Concorde
  a wide and spindled planisphere,
  and St. Germain-des-Prés another
  church.

Weathering your dreams,
bronze Paris of the doorknobs
turns into the turning stage
called *here* that stays the same
as everywhere right now.
On that
quick stage a man keeps happening.
From Paris to Paris to Paris,
the only life he knows
is anywhere and always coming
true . . .
His name is *you.*

II

Seafall

In the Order of Disappearance

This blue is where the bull shark
  hunts.
        You listen to the smell
of seafall, touch what drowning
means and taste the thud
of salty alleluias on the beach.
A fish-rib comb proclaims
  that all distinctions fade
  in the diminishing.
             Spar and seawood
  rhyme like skeleton with skeleton.
An audience of one, you fish
  the air for sounds, for differences.
For differences?
        They're of the land
where everything from flint to rosewood
steadies in the stopped psalms
of Moses.
        Only the namers change,
bequeathing to the last minorities
their sounded pictures, pictured
songs and other echoes of the not
yet thinkable.
        Their carvings chant.
Their songs remind you that forever's
  when it's always now.
          Their gospels
say they primed for death
by trying to imagine how they'd look
asleep.
        Unnamable, they've disappeared
with cavemen, gypsies, sellers

of insurance, saviors, kids
and numbered kings with all
their bastardies.
                They seem to you
like swords honed down, honed
down until there's nothing left
to hone, like grenadella branches
offered to a blaze, like rocks
erased by sledging waterdrops
repeated and repeated.
                Married
to the moon, this womb of blue
and bone encircles you like zero's
tomb.
          It tells you that by knowing
what you're not, you come
to what you are, and what
you are is just a comma
to the waves.
              You wait for promises
to prove that you were here.
Undisappearing yet, you wage
yourself against the noosing war
of water and its whirlpool kill.
The script is in the sand.
                Your toemarks
say the tide scrolls out and in,
the waves keep hilling, milling,
chilling, and the whirlpools win.

Castaway

Purple, navy, aquamarine
  and emerald, the combers tumble
  brown to Byblos and its walls.
Each wave shatters in blustery
  applause across the reefs, then surfs
  the shallows like a sprinter lunging
  for a tape and pitching through it.
Wave on wave reshuffles, cuts
  and deals the shore its solitaire
  of shells, leafmuck or seavines
  webbed around a fin.
                Blink,
  and everything's sucked back to sea
  again or pummeled undersand.
A tanker on the skyline nudges
  eastward like a target on a rifle
  range.
         Inch by inch its reasons
  tow it out of sight.
              Or was it
  ever there?
        The sea keeps dealing.

Between Wars

After the twelve-day storm, the ocean
  settles like a sheet tugged taut.
Instead of being something
  to survive, the dawn is simply
  one more dawn.
                You lollygag
  on deck, deal poker in the hold
  and shave the beard you now find
  time to shave.
              The mate remembers
  that his ulcer ought to bother him.
Bo's'ns hate their officers again,
  and stokers use the same, quick
  nouns to damn the food that they
  had used to pray the winds away.
By noon you wish those weathers
  back when you were just afraid
  to be afraid, when every watch
  meant death or breath, when nothing
  but the storm was real.
                 You brag
  that it takes storms to make the sea
  the sea, and sailors sailors.
By night you dream the opposite.
You merely lack the seamanship
  to cope with peaceful waters.

Saltpulse

When waves attack the sandy
  capes of all the continents
  like young, white bulls at dawn
  and old, black bulls at dusk,
  you can't pretend they're raging
  for the deaf or charging at the blind.
Rush by rise by rush
  they gallop in until you gallop
  with them.
              Landlocked or rocketing,
  you're of the sea that stays
  three-fourths of everything.
                    Your blood,
  your spittle and your sweat all
  taste of it.
          It mints the mock
  brine of your son's tears.
It salts the kisses that you give
  your wife.
          At sea your sex
  and seed remember it.
                 Ashore
  in space, you watch the turning
  sands go all at once awash
  and settle darkly as a sub
  submerging.
          Hemispheres dissolve.
Uplands become lowlands,
  and lowlands sink until the Baltic
  and the Caribbean touch.

                                    Then peaks
and poles go under, and the whole
sealevel planet dwindles
to a glint in the swing of a ring
of the king of all Calders
floating in the fathoms of the sun.

Regardless

In this clear sea the drowned
  are who they were again.
Under the night's chalk sun
  they walk the waves like Jesuses
  and chant they'll never die
  until you die.
             They lead you,
  lead you farther, lead you farther
  seaward every moon . . .
                But this is
Sunday, and the island named Regardless
offers you its green.
             The wild
  pig keeps to the hills.
              Pineapple
  and pimento spice the breezes
  while you salt and sizzle lamblegs
  over charcoals on the beach.
               By dawn
  you dance the sailor's dance of
  Rhodes, Ukrainian circles
  and the jumps and leaps of Muscovy.
The embers throb like orange hearts,
  burn slowly gray and crumble.
Wading east, you fling
  the lamb bones out to sea
  and sing the morning's yellow moon
  by thirds above the oceanline
  until it bobs the whole way
  up to keep the drowned at bay.

To Dive

The bed you ride on rides
   the deck that rides the waves.
Porthole breezes cool your pillow.
Ice water in a pitcher tilts
   to the schooner's pitch, roll
   and yaw.
              Above you on the dance
floor, an orchestra completes
its sambas.
             Stomping down the hall
in shower clogs, a boy whistles
the Cuban national anthem
flat until his mother quiets
him in Arabic.
             Then, midnight.
Coffee, peppercorns and copra
   ripen in the hold.
             Brine
swills where the ship's halves
fuse into the keel, and underneath
the keel a manta plunges
like a bomber's shadow through
a cloud of smelt.
             Floating
on your sheeted raft, you dream
a dive through halls and holds
and hulls . . .
             You surface breathless
to the naked bride you've loved
a thousand times before.
             Icily,
your bedside pitcher glimmers
amber with the fire of your skins.
Already you are gripping, grappling
   for the first time, again.

III

The Mute Riot of Everything

Mattering

Not men of state.
                    This century
        owes more to Thomas Alva
        Edison and Henry Ford
        than any politician will admit.
For proof, imagine unilluminated
        San Francisco or a trek
        by any means but car in January
        from Chicago to the Maine woods.
Not poets.
                    Considering the lot,
        you'll find two possible Beethovens,
        four Ravels, no Bachs, one
        definite Mozart and sundry Gershwins.
The rest are so many word-whittlers
        keeping the world safe for sounds,
        sales, sodomy or one another.
Not goddesses.
                    The girl DiMaggio
        was man enough to bury and remember
        ended nude beneath a sheet
        with morgue-tags wired to her thumb-toes.
Not the chosen state of mind.
Nor anything that's arrogant
        in victory and, in defeat, self-
        pitying.
                    Nor anyone who claims
        that everybody's guilty, but no one's
        responsible.
                    Nor any creed that chants
        exclusion in the name of God
        and offers all the answers but no questions.

Not uniforms, invisible or visible.
All uniforms demand allegiances.
Allegiances presume obedience.
Obedience assumes there's strength
    in numbers, which is weakness multiplied.
Not time or place.
                    If all above
    the earth is sky, you breathe
    the drowning sky until your breathing's
    over, but the sky goes on.
What matters then?
                    Another
    faith ago, you said you sought
    no future but the given day
    to live your dying in the risen
    world.
            What mattered then
    keep mattering.
                    No matter how
    you try, you can't deny that life
    might matter more than dying
    day by day until the day
    you die—not matter why.

In Convoy

Highways from here, a skunk,
  run over at the neck, stares on.
Like quartz in coal, its eyes
  still multiply all headlights
  and the moon by two.
                    Pastures away,
  a rabbit nibbles peach leaves,
  and a single daisy times a million
  on a mountain shows the stars
  what daisypower means.
                  Your
  neighborhood's a clutch of prairie
  schooners sailing straight
  through midnight and beyond.
                    Each
  attic whispers by without
  an SOS.
          The semaphore of streetlamp
  after streetlamp punctuates and codes
  the dark.
          Antares flashes pintip-
  red above a television aerial.
Seatight inside your shiphouse,
  you have no port except to stay
  afloat as long as possible.
                On watch,
  you puff your briar and inscribe
  ink entries in a log.
            Your pen's
  your mightier sword.
             Its drawn point
  duels the mute riot of everything.

Victorious Losses

Too busy saying what you choose,
  your words rush straight ahead
  like some unsteady solo
  in the key of reason.
                    No sharps,
  no flats, nothing left to syncopation,
  not a hint of dazzle.
                    Predictably,
  the final words that end
  the final lines must kiss—
  like this.
                    Dominoes!
                    The world
  keeps waiting for a voice to tell
  it what it means while you
  play dominoes.
                    Even your days
  are dominoes.
                    You count your steps.
Each dawn you brush your up-teeth
  down and then your down-teeth
  up.
          The spaced and slowly
  sinking heartbeat of a deathbell
  sobers every ear but yours.
Remember Ivan's words on death?
"The dead outnumber us—we all
  must join that last majority—
  to die is simply democratic."
Could you have uttered that
  and slapped your knee and laughed?

Remember too the girl you quietly
   desired and thought you loved
   but never made love to?
                    Facing
   the possibility of pleasure
   and the certainty of guilt, you
   backed into the future like a thief.
At worst you're still a puritan,
   still ready to retreat into a simpler
   world that's always waiting to receive
   the man you think you are.
At best you live by Goethe's creed
   that thought begins in private,
   character in public.
                   Alone
   with dreams you can't refute
   and wants you never want to want,
   you turn to words until
   you turn into the words you write.
Your metronome collapses, and your
   lines unrhyme while you go on
   committing poetry, that holy crime.

Flying Down the Dream

It's like tobogganing.
                              You scud
   the frosted cupolas of clouds
   instead of snow, thumping
   over bumps of turbulence
   but otherwise at peace.
                              Tan
   coffee seesaws in your plexicup.
Across the aisle three sailors
   argue over five-card stud.
Beside you in the windowseat,
   a fourth unfolds by thirds
   a centerpage of pelvis, breasts
   and then the rest of Miss July . . .
Five minutes west of home, you try
   imagining what's going on below.
Your son should be in school.
Your wife might be addressing
   envelopes.
                      Aging apart from them,
   you're like Ulysses viewing Ithaca
   from heaven . . .
                              Thunderstatic
   shakes the fuselage like flak,
   and down you drop.
                              Buzzers buzz,
   and seatbelt signs blink red
   in lower-case American and French.
Spilt, your coffee tans
   the sunspared ass of Miss July.
The galley's hardware rattles
   like a carnival of cans behind
   a wedding car.

                    You tell yourself
        what's happening's not happening.
You bless and hold your holy
        breath.
                    Everyone aboard
        becomes your brother and your sister
        all at once.
                    You think about
        your wife and son without you . . .
Swallowing the choking from your ears,
        you watch the cabin lensing
        back to focus, caliber by caliber.
A stewardess appears, all smiles
        and amnesia.
                    Over the intercom
        the captain's "really sorry about that."
The sailor at your elbow shakes
        your coffee from his page and pages
        back before he pages on.
                    And you?
You wait until the steadily ascending
        planet turns into the underrolling
        runway at the ending . . .
                    And you breathe.

The Bearing

Heavy from her steady bellying,
    the mare comes due.
                    No memory
    of ten Kentuckies or the horse farms
    east of Buffalo prepares you
    for the silk of that first fur.
You've seen the Easter foals stilting
    in toy gallops by their almost
    inattentive mothers.
                    You've known
    from watching what the breeding
    of Arabia will hone from all
    that spindliness: in weeks, the fetlocks
    shapelier; in months, the girth below
    the withers sinewed like a harp;
    in years, the stance and prancing
    that will stop a crowd.
But now the colt's nose nudging
    for horsemilk nullifies a dream
    to come of stallions.
                    Now
    it is enough to know that something
    can arrive so perfectly and stand
    upright among so many fallen
    miracles and, standing, fill
    the suddenly all sacred barn
    with trumpets and a memory of kings.

Beheaded

You watch your head take shape
  from the collar up.
                The sculptor's
  rosewood spoons discover
  in the clay your graygreen
  face (three-quarter-sized)
  until it's there.
             Across
  your forehead, sunlight slashes
  like a chain of lightning flashing
  zigzags through the sculptor's fingers.
Dead in your posing flesh,
  you come alive in clay.
You're not the everlasting father
  of a son, not the penman
  of chucked pages, not the traveler
  who trailed two fingers in the Seine
  so he could say he trailed
  two fingers in the Seine.
             Instead,
  you're any head without a trunk.
Plattered in neckblood, clots
  and beard, you keep the Baptist's
  look of boredom and surprise.
Or are you Thomas of the tower
  after Henry made his choice?
Unlike the head of Holofernes
  heisted by the hair, your head's
  at peace.
           With nothing more
  to lose, you speak to listeners
  three centuries away.

47

Listen.
You can almost hear what you
   are saying.

            Or are you
still the singing shepherd
gored in ambush by a pig
because you loved the queen
of sorrowing?

            You watch the witches
of the mountain make a beanbag
of your head before they feed it
bleeding to a stream.

            Downstream,
the current reddens to a river,
and the river reddens to the sea
that reddens slowly outward
to the hemispheres . . .

            Your sitting ends.
While you unpose and stretch,
the sculptor packs the fingered clay
with poultices.

            Under damp burlap,
the head keeps thinking, thinking.

A City Made Sacred Because Your Son's Grandfather Died in It

Your father in a wheelchair slouches
   steeply to his stroked-out side.
Your son wheels for the final
   time his final grandfather.
And you, who've walked this street
   so many times you know
   the slope and crack of every
   sidewalk square, just walk
   behind.
           You ask your son
(or is it just your son?)
   to slow things down.
Your father flicks his good
   right hand to say he can't
   accept but won't deny what's
   happened, that not accepting
   what is unacceptable is all
   life meant or means to him.
You want to hold his other
   hand and squeeze it back
   to life until the doctors
   and their facts relent.
           The doctors
and their facts go on.
           So do
the unaffected riders in the numbered
buses.
      So does the whole
damn city that becomes no more
than just a place to live
and die in now.

49

              The more you walk,
the less you know the street
you knew.
                The less you know,
the more the curbs become
opposing shores. The street
is suddenly the river no man
steps in twice or finally outswims.
Midway between your father
and your son, you feel yourself
drawn in and on and under.

The Day Your Son Was Born, It Is

Last night you saw it hooded,
   silent, sipping from the saucer
   of a child's skull a child's
   blood.
            Tonight it puts aside
   that holy wine and leaves you
   falling like a dreamer in a void.
It is the darker twin of love.
It comes when you are least
   or most prepared.
                  It is the viper
   in your sock, the sand that bogs
   you to a stop, the scream
   you strain to scream but never
   scream.
            Awake, you ask
   the night if what you dream
   is what all fathers dream.
Your midnight house keeps talking
   to itself.
            A nightlight paints
   a gargoyle on the ceiling while
   you smoke another inch from yesterday's
   cigar.
            For minutes you mistake it
   in the smoke until you recognize
   the hood, the face averted
   and the rest in shadow.
                        Silent,
   it stays as near as air.

                    It bids
at baccarat with something in another
hood.
                Call that its mirror trick.
Call that its solitaire for two
    or give it any name that shows
    how fear and fear's illusions
    are the same.
                    As long as you
    go on, so does the game.

The Duel That Is Vertical

Nearing the world of nine
  Novembers, he astounds you,
  makes you dream of reruns,
  maddens you for missing what
  can only happen once or never.
Cheek against your arm, he asks
  you how we hear—exactly how?
You talk of waves, vibrations,
  tympany and then give up.
Lately you give up on more
  and more—on God, on death,
  on whether goldfish sleep
  or where the sky stops.
                Before
undoubtful doubts, you stand
on ignorance.
            You stall the vaccination
of the facts.
            You answer mystery
with mystery.
            Headed as a pair
for sleep, you play a game
that knights you in the name
of wonder.
            Flying buses
stand for jets—freighters
are sea-trucks—applause is happy
noise, and so on.
            He leads.
You counter.
            Almost asleep,
he tells you how he dreams

of chasing lions through Alaska
on his bike.
                    You ask him
if he's heard there are
no lions in Alaska.
                    He says
there are if he can dream there are.
Before undreamers undeceive him,
    you believe him, dream by dream.

The Poem That Wouldn't Soar

Cramped as signatures, your written
and rewritten words keep missing
what you mean.
                    Your paper crawls
with black graffiti chanced
into designs.
                    Like Moslem art
they blaze with order but cannot
take off.
                    Frowning, you put
aside your pen as any general
might table his surrendered sword.
Why fight this servitude?
                              Why tell
any empty page the way you walk
in France or how sink water slowly
corkscrews in a whirlpool down
a drain?
                    Between the questions
and the shrug, your pen stays mute,
your page lies heavy with its
epitaphs, and all your soarings
die the death of feathers . . .
                              Later,
your son selects your failure
of a poem as his own and folds it
into wings.
                    You watch him
walk it to the wind and aim it
like an archer at the sun.

                              Flung,
the paper that was merely paper
inked with your defeats becomes
the poem it was meant to be,
and, like a horse with wings as free
and wild as the air, takes off.

The Worst Dancers Watch Their Feet

You have to watch your feet,
   but Anne has feet that think
   and memorize.
                  Name any country,
   and her feet are instant citizens.
In Stratford once she danced
   with Englishmen and Englishwomen,
   learning as she stepped until
   her steps were English as the songs.
In Lebanon she showed them how.
In Greece she passed for Greek
   and passes still.
                  In Italy
   and Spain, the same.
                  Bazouki,
   tamburitza, oud, guitar,
   all drums from barrel thumpings
   to the marching tympany of fingers
   on a tabletop—it makes no
   difference.
                  Her feet have birthright
   keys to every alphabet
   while yours speak only in American.
If music were the sea, you'd
   thrash to save yourself
   and slowly drown, while she
   would dance each wave alone
   in her ballet without a splash
   or ripple or a last look down.

Night Letter to America on Switzerland's Independence Day

What Calvin called the body
   of this death is memory enough
   for you.
            Which memory?
                     If you
   remembered that, you'd prophesy
   just how you'll die.
                  Ignorant,
   you face your term and time
   the way a pregnant women
   faces labor, certain of the *if*
   but doubtful of the *how* and *when*
   and always of the *why*.
                        Bearing
   with a different *why*, you labor on.
No fate prefigures yours, not Rilke
   in Muzot, not Henry of the last
   addresses, not bombed commandos
   trucked like carcass beef
   from skirmishes, not Charles de Gaulle
   at solitaire (at solitaire!) convulsed
   and taken.
            Anticipating or remembering,
   you're left with words.
                        Assured
   that what you write will matter
   more in Europe than in all
   the States, you see your country
   flawed with hollows.
                     Half
   its citizens have never learned
   its creeds.

                    What's left of Jefferson's
once "solid . . . independent yeomanry"
is paid to grow, then burn
its crops.
                    Good lakes and better
clouds are fouled with the filth
of mills, and men whose clothes
are costumes bark the day's bad
news as if their mouths were anuses . . .
Beneath Geneva's current carnival
    of seven centuries of fireworks,
    you see the light.
                    Americans are not
America—not yet.
                    The dynamo
of Henry Adams pulses like a tumor
in their skulls.
                    The motor runs and runs.
Dying's a stoppage; love,
    a diversion; sickness, a delay;
    children, an inconvenience.
What's left?
                    If happiness is not
the same as freedom, love,
children and the art of work,
what is it?
                    The Swiss respond
by being Swiss as certainly
as all their clocks repeat themselves
two times a day.
                    You wish
your countrymen that much
of someone else's history.
                    You stay
so in this pilgrim's telegram
and post it to be opened in event
of death.
                    You never mention whose.

59

Birth of a Poet

The words mean war.
                    They tell
you to forget your first and last
allegiances and every syllable
you've ever said.
                    You ask them
what they came to offer, and they
order you to offer them yourself
this minute at the latest.
They add that they're an army
looking for a general.
                    When you
confess you're not a general
and never were, they batter you
with numbers, topple the pope
of your conscience, ignore white
flags and claim you for themselves.
Jabbering, they butt skulls.
Like boys they don't know why
they're doing what they're doing
even while they're doing it.
They leave you jailed within yourself
but free to move.
                    You think
of nothing else but them.
                    You learn
too late that that's their strategy.
By then you know each word
by name.
                    Tortured by attention,
even the most recalcitrant becomes

convivial, tactless, willing
to swap secrets.
                    The horseplay
 stops, and all the words fall
in and wait for your commands
to march them to the front.
                         Nobody
balks.
          Suddenly the battle that was
on in force is just as suddenly
suspended.
               Seeking something
of a victory from such a total
self-defeat, you look around
to find what's left of you.
And you are still looking . . .

IV

The Fiftieth of January

The Only Comedy

This play's a spider.
                    Centering
a small circumference of legs,
it sidles in a wild skidaddle
everywhere ahead.
                    It knits
from its own spit a snowflake-
web that's like a clock
with hands for everything
from seconds to millennia.
                                        Its
leading character keeps time
by centuries, which means
he speaks and gestures s-l-o-w-l-y.
The other characters are people
of the minute-hand and second-hand
respectively.
                    Nakedly alike,
they change each time their stage
directions and their costumes
turn them into roles.
                         One-liners,
uttered quickly, are the most
they say.
            "There are no blondes
in China."
                "Gooney birds
in take-off run like nuns
in galoshes."
                    "Theology's
the gospel of the unbeliever."

65

"Bards of a feather flock
together."
All this by way
of hiding from an audience
that isn't there the play's
apparent lack of plot.
Its own event, it keeps on
happening.
As for the cast,
the female lead resents
the ingenue, the understudies
dream to be directors,
and the chorus sees what everybody
sees and says so in pentameters.
The voice coach tells them all,
"Your language must be clear
as poetry and yet as irresistible
as gossip."
Each time an actor
claims the stage is overheated,
someone in the rafters shouts,
"You're 98.6 inside, and we're
way short of that."
On colder days he says,
"You're 98.6 inside, and that's
a furnace when you think of it—
so, think of it!"
Meanwhile
a picket crosses with a placard
reading, "Men in gas masks
look like walking pigs."
A scaffold
falls backstage.
Damage
minor . . .

Halfway through her major
scene, the ingenue departs
to use the bathroom.
                              "Come back
here!" bellows the director.
"Wherever I go is here!"
she says and goes . . .
                              Excepting
a poetic moment now and then,
the critics find the characters
monotonous, the dialogue disjointed
and the scenery pedestrian.
One pundit writes, "The plot's
as fresh as a sinkful of sour
socks."
                   Later he likens
the crowded stage to a crock
of sand spiked with butts.
Outimaged and outquipped,
the playwright hurries to revise
the script.
                   "What script?"
demands the chorus, abandoning
pentameters to speak the truth.
By now the hero has progressed
from slow to stock-still.
                              He dies
the passion of the totally misunderstood,
which means he dies like everyone,
which means his heroism's dubious
at best.
                   More scaffolds fall
backstage.
                   The one-liners
carry one, regardless.

                      "Photographs
are epitaphs in transit."
                                  "Peace
makes money, and money makes war."
No one can answer how the play
   began or where it's going
   or how long the run will be.
The only thing that's certain
   is the stage, the changing players
   and the sets . . .
                      At last report,
   the show's still on.

Only the New Branches Bloom

For Grace, 7/19/78

Denying what it means to doubt,
  this year's forsythias unfold
  and flood the air with yellow
answers.
          They say it's time
I opened up, time I learned
French, time I liked less
and loved more, time
I listened to the sun, time
I made time.
          Why not?
Can days of making sense
  of days that make no sense
  make sense?
          If nothing's sure
but nothing's sure, then reading
Montesquieu must wait.
Preparing for my enemies must
  wait.
          And gravity the hurrier
must wait because forsythias
are happening.
          They make me
turn my back on facts,
insurance policies, inoculations.
wire barbed or braided,
bodyguards and all the folderol
of fear.
          They say that this
year's blossoms will outlive
the lasting death of Mars.
There are no flowers on the stars.

The Time That Will Happen Because

Stripped like drowned torches,
    the oaks stop being oaks—
not a leaf left and none
to come until the amnesty
of March.
            Like so much
history, the leaves insist
that I assemble them.
                    They say
tomorrow's yesterday.
                    They turn
to deathrot underfoot or feather
out of reach before I rack
my rake and let the crosswinds
broom them into mulch.
                    Unless
I think of history, what's history?
Half luxury, half penalty, it
whittles me away like sink
soap worn to a wafer.
                    It says
my life's a leaf predestined
for the rake, the wind, the match.
It makes me understand why
    Icarus went sailing for the sun.
At odds with gravity, he chose
    to prove that history is what
a man must make and thus
not history at all.
                    Among
November's leaves and lives,
I'm Icarus enough to know

that history's a watch still ticking
on a dead man's wrist.
                                    I silence
it by gambling with the wind
the way a singer draws
a breath and gives it back
as music.
                    Airborne, I feel
a poem burst all through me
all at once.
                    The words parade
like new and naked brides
from countries where the calendars
are empty, and the clocks show
just one hand that points
forever at the center of the sun.

Leafing

Bagged and burned, they turn
  into the only smoke that's worth
  the tasting.
                Woods revert
  to wood as I, their janitor,
  rake up the year.
                Cleansed,
  cleansed to my tree of bones
  and savoring the blown tobacco
  of November, I recall Chateaubriand's
  "Forests precede civilizations,
  and deserts follow them."
Disturbing comments for a ballpoint
  era where psychiatry's the state
  religion, and the prize of prizes
  is a champagne shampoo
  in the locker room.
                My woods
  are far from forests, but I know
  real deserts when I see them.
So, I work my bonewood rake,
  leafing for reasons to repudiate
  Chateaubriand.
                The answer's
  in the trees.
                Shorn to their shells,
  they'll wait the winter out
  and start all over when
  the time is right.
                By then
  the desert's prize and predecessors
  will have gone the way of smoke.
As long as there's a leaf, there's hope.

Yellow Delicious

From branching chandeliers they bell,
  drop and dribble still
  as tennis balls.
            The overripe
batter the ground in a smatter
of pulp.
           The rest, malshaped
as peppers cored by wasps
or worms but coming crookedly
to term, swing high
and green . . .
            I did my summer
best with watersoaks
and sprays.
           I planted stakes
of vitamins full circle
at the drip line.
            Nothing worked . . .
Shrugging, I watch the leaves
  curl brittle in September's fire.
I see the limbs and crown
  revert to architecture that will
  sleep the snowfalls and persist.
That's mystery enough for me.
Next summer means another tree.

Statues from a January River

For Grace, 11/12/79

After the sculptors' cuts
   and chiselings, ice hunks
   the size of small garages
   rise as horses, chariots
   or bells.
         Shining like chandeliers,
   they prove the pyramids were wrong
   to rival what the rain alone
   remembers of our wars,
   our kingdoms and our withering
   cathedrals.
         Better a loss
   to the first crocus than to build
   what's meant for banishing by winter
   after winter of the wind.
              Better
   the handiwork that chisels clear
   as dreams or tears just once—
   just once before the vanishing.

The Tropics of the Snow

I towel down before a gawking
   goldfish.
               Two nudes, we size
   each other up.
               Nude also
   in its crock, a winter flower
   wakes me to the alphabet
   of silence.
               From flesh to fin
   to petals thinner than a flake
   of frost, we're of a clan.
Tomorrow when I talk in clothes
   and other languages, I'll try
   remembering what I remember
   now . . .
               That girl in Nice . . .
Anointed for the sun, her body's
   naked face became
   a tan magnetic field
   that drew me in.
               A windowpane
   away from filibusters of the snow,
   I dream she meets my goldfish
   stare again.
               Her fluent nipples
   look at me in French.
And I, with nothing on my mind
   but breasts with nothing on,
   wake up and listen with my skin.

Sexes

She or someone like her woke
   the wasps in David's, Caesar's,
   Casanova's brain.
               Stung,
   the loins took over, and the plot
   outgrew the musk behind her
   yawning kiss, the heft in hand
   of either breast, the muted
   thumps of bellies in a bed.
Later, the truths . . .
              That she
   exclaims what she thinks
   when she thinks it.
              That she
   proclaims all photographs unflattering.
That what she lacks in looks
   she compensates with furs,
   colognes, low lights and gems.
By then David as king
   forgets his first inseminations
   and composes psalms of some
   merit.
          Caesar remembers
   Cleopatra in the way old generals
   recall an older battle's
   oldest wound.
          And Casanova
   at his memoirs dreams each night
   all night of what was once
   better than caviar and more available.

The Toys

Wing to wing, they bake
  in weather that can sizzle bacon
  on their stars.
                       Fighters, bombers,
  trainers—Arizona stores them all
  unrusting in a prophecy of yesterday.
West by half the Pacific, the holy
  salvage of another *Arizona*
  consecrates Pearl Harbor like a church . . .
If wreckages were pages, nothing
  could book them.
                   Cain's garbage
  mines the Baltic, fouls
  forty years of bracken near
  Cassino, spoils Guam's lagoon.
What were these havocs to their crews
  but new toys for an old game?
As facts left over from a fact,
  they speak for history ahead
  of all that history remembers
  to predict about the tactics of our kind.
Cain's rock and rocket
  leave us nothing new to find.
In North America the oldest skull's
  a woman's, brained from behind.

Living's How We Die and Vice Versa

Stitched with bridges, the river
  changes under crossbows
  arched at thunder, highways
  hung from steel harps,
  trestles for clocked pullmans
  and the chainlink freights.
                        The rust's
already happening.
                       Only the river
stays the same by flowing different
every different minute to the sea.
Like any follower, I read my fortune
  in the rivertow.
                Bridging half
a century, my body slackens
while it keeps on going.
                  Resign
or rest, and what remains
but slowing down?
                Rely
on heaven as the nay of now,
and what's today but yesterday
plus nothing?
            Resist, and I
might leave some echo of myself
in blood or book before the last
assassinating clock strikes no.
The son I lucked from God
leaves me no living to regret.
The world I make by seeing it
  and make all over just by saying
  so or writing so is all the world
  I need.

But seen or seen again,
it goes.
   And, gone, it shows
that when we go, we're everywhere
at once and always nearer
for the going.
   Even my pipesmoke
prophesies that much of mine
or anyone's goodbye.
   It twists
and dawdles through the air before
it rivers down beneath a window
sill and turns into the sky.

An Almanack of Solitude

Outside—slag of the sky,
   slush seasoned to the tint
   of sinkwater, tundra
   by the neighborhood, streets where
   pawprint, bootprint and the Greek
   keys of tire treads endure
   like slogans in cement . . .
                 The date?
The fiftieth of January.
             Nothing
  melts.
       Toughened into crusts,
  the snow scabs to the ground.
Ices on shingles slide
  and slim to dagger points.
Entombed, a million tulips wait
  like princesses for kisses of the sun
  to waken them . . .
              I ache
  for Anne in Taormina where
  the rainbows arch on mint
  and lemons, and the sun's a prince
  with light enough for all
  the green in Sicily.
             Trapped
  by the old snow of slow
  days and slower nights,
  I weary of this winter of the moon.
The primavera sky, where is it?
And where the smile that can solve
  the waiting and the weather and the words?

Long Distance Isn't

Separated by a sea, two shores,
   the clans of Vercingetorix, the Brenner
   Pass, the boot of Italy
   from just below the knee to halfway
   down the calf, we nix them all
   by phone.
             Our voices kiss.
Who cares if the Atlantic bashes
   Maine, Land's End or Normandy?
We leapfrog hemispheres the way
   the mind cavorts through God-knows-what
   millennia, what dynasties, what
   samples of our kind from
   australopithecus to Charlie Chaplin.
The body's place?
             Cross latitude
   by longitude, and it is there.
The body's age?
            Count up
   from birth or back from death,
   and it is there.
           But words?
We launch them out like vows
   against the wind.
             Creating what we are,
   they wing through seas and continents
   and make us more than elegies
   to yesterday.
           Forget the cost.
Talk louder and ignore the static.
Pretend we're walking through the dark.

Don't stop.
                    Don't stop or look
behind you.
                    As long as you
keep talking, I can find you.

Dublin Twilight

From Parnell's statue to O'Connell's
  I can smell America's sixties
  when the center did not hold.
Priests resemble priests, and nuns
   are nuns.
               A Shaw play runs
  at the Abbey.
                  Arrayed in rows
  beside the *Summa Theologica*,
Joyce sells well while his bones
  age in Zurich.
                 "No nation
  has the right to fix the boundary
  to the march of a nation," wrote Parnell
  before the troubles and the tans.
Locked in this city of drizzle,
   soot and kindness, the only
   march is traffic and shoppers.
Alighting on O'Connell's granite
   scalp, a pigeon perches
   like some dirty dove of hope.
It stares and stays while Yeats'
   lion-bodied saviors battle
   in Belfast, and a Liffey sidewalk
   slogan damns the pope.

The Silence at the Bottom of the Well

It's been expecting me so long
 that I feel late.
     Dropped
 stones are what it's thirsty for,
 and I've come armed . . .
        I hear
 the ghosts of splashes plummet
 upward like the tired swallows
 of a heart near death.
       If I
 could dunk and hoist a bucket,
 I would taste what mountain
 brooks remember of the snow.
Instead, I whisper down
 my name, my name, my name
 and listen as it yoyos
 in a rounding echo back,
 back, back . . .
      Below the parapet
 the swirling walls dive
 farther down than I can dream.
Deeper, where night and water
 meet, the moon of the assassins
 waits for yesterday, and never sleeps.

The Time It Is in Sofia

No whistles now, no horns . . .
A thousand moons float flat
   on rain lakes, bobbing
   as the wind bends over them.
Birdchant and dogtalk wrangle
   in the almost dawn.
                     They surface
   all at once like lights
   that blink awake on dark oceans.
I squint for them as I
   might listen to my pulse
   or to a woman humming naked
   in another room.
                  The only
   other sentries are the stars . . .
What is it to the stars if I
   imagine watchmen somewhere
   chewing silent bread
   and silent cheese, a farmer
   somewhere silencing a stallion,
   lovers somewhere sleeping off
   the sweet pain that ends
   in ecstasy?
             My dreams rain
   down into the holy wisdom
   of the facts.
               Beyond the Russian
Embassy, a pair of soccer
players walk a soccer
ball between them as they sing.

The stars are light enough
        to see them home with still
        the taste of victory and vodka
        in their eyes.
                        They disappear
but stay the way skywriting
disappears but stays forever
in the mind's sure sky.
                                For years
I'll hear them clapping in Bulgarian.

Maps for a Son Are Drawn As You Go

I say what Lindbergh's father
  said to Lindbergh: "One boy's
  a boy; two boys are half
  a boy; three boys are no
  boy at all."
              Which helps explain
  why Lindbergh kept his boyishness
  for life, which meant he stayed
  himself, which means a lot.
What else is destiny?
             After
  you learn that governments lie
  and happiness is undefinable
  and death has no patience,
  you'll understand me.
             Meanwhile
  the ignorant but well informed
  will try to keep you mute
  as a shut book.
             Forecasters of the best
  and worst will hurry to retreat
  infallibly into the future.
             Ministers
  who talk on cue with God
  will weigh you down like serious
  furniture.
             Assume that what
  you lose to such distractions
  you will gain in strength.
By then you'll learn that all
  you know will help you less
  than how you think.

                              The rest
        is memory, and memory's the graveyard
        of the mind as surely as tomorrow
        is its myth.
                              Nowhere but the time
        at hand is when you'll see
        that God's geometry is feast
        enough.
                              Within the world's
        closed circles, everything's
        the sum of halves that rhyme.
From coconuts to butterflies
        to lovers knotted on the soft
        battlefield of any bed, the halves
        add up to one, and every
        one remembers where it came
        from as a trumpet note
        recalls the song it was a part of
        and the listeners who heard it
        and were changed.
                              What Lindbergh's
        father meant and what I mean
        are two roads to the same
        country.
                              Knowing how long
        it takes us to be young, he left
        his son some clues to get
        his bearings by.
                              And so do I.